Hope
for
TODAY'S
FAMILIES

TIMELESS ADVICE
from a FAVORITE PREACHER

~

Hope
for
TODAY'S
FAMILIES

W. Frank Harrington

PEACHTREE PRESBYTERIAN CHURCH PRESS

Atlanta, Georgia

1999

*For more information about
the W. Frank Harrington Legacy Project,
which seeks to preserve Dr. Harrington's work
for future generations, visit http://www.wfhlegacy.org.*

℘♥

Scripture quotations are taken from the Holy Bible, New Living Translation, © 1996. Used by permission of Tyndale House Publishers, Inc., Wheaton, IL 60189. All rights reserved.

International Standard Book Number: 1-929716-00-1

Executive editor: Susan Harrington Potter
Editors: Betty Wyatt and Jeff Potter
Copy editor: Michael Trotman
Cover and text design and production: Jeff Potter

Typeset in Cloister

Printed in the United States of America by Sheridan Books

10 9 8 7 6 5 4 3 2 1

CONTENTS

INTRODUCTION

Watching My Family

vii

I

What Is a Family?

1

II

Single Parents: I Salute Them

23

III

The Blended Family

Yours, Mine, and Sometimes Ours!

39

IV

Too Much or Too Little?

What We Must Give Our Kids

53

V

The Challenges Our Kids Face

67

VI

How Could One Abuse a Child?

79

VII

Don't Give Up!

Advice for Parents and Teenagers

93

VIII

Promises That Every Parent Can Make

111

ABOUT THE AUTHOR

123

INTRODUCTION

Watching My Family

ONE SUNDAY MORNING, I arrived at my church early and was sitting in my office going over my sermon one more time. As I looked out the window, I noticed a steady stream of cars coming into the parking lot, and as the members of my congregation began to move into the church, the idea for this book was born.

I have been privileged to serve the Peachtree Presbyterian Church in Atlanta for almost thirty years, and I have come to know and love its members as my own family. That Sunday morning I watched one young couple whom I had baptized after their first confirmation classes. I watched them grow and mature and later had the privilege of performing their wedding. As they came into the church that Sunday, they were bringing their newborn baby to be baptized. That started me to thinking about the tremendous responsibility, and the fantastic opportunity, before them.

I watched a wonderful older couple get out of their car and walk toward the Sunday School wing with their grandchild. He now lived with them, and they were once again experiencing the joy and challenges of raising a child. Circumstances presented them with the possibility of seeing this grandchild raised by strangers, and they opened their arms, their hearts, and their home. The love and happiness they were experiencing showed on their faces.

Another young father came in with his three children. I had recently conducted the funeral service for the mother. His steps were slow, but his shoulders were squared as he faced the future with determination. My heart went out to him, for the road ahead would be lonely, but I was filled with pride as he carried on. I knew that he received support from his friends and reminded myself to call on him during the coming week.

Almost right behind him came a newly divorced mother of two. She was struggling to accept rejection and get on with her life. She hadn't worked in years, but now was seeking a job. I feared that most of the financial support of her family would come from her. There were adjustments ahead not only for her, but also for those precious children. I made a note in my calendar to call a couple of the members of Peachtree to discuss helping her find employment — and to remind our day-care director to be alert for any signs that the children might need some special care and help.

I heard a child crying and looked out to see a young mother and father bringing their new baby into the nursery. Several years before, I had gone to them at the hospital as they received the news from the doctor that their son had Down's syndrome. He explained the prognosis to them and suggested that they might consider more professional care in an institution. Almost simultaneously they looked at each other, and with one voice stated that they would provide the love and care needed at their home as long as they were physically able to do so. This young boy was walking into church carrying his Bible, and he was so proud of his new sister. His parents faced the strain of caring for a child with special needs, and they exhibited their faith and hope for the future by bringing another child into their family.

There came a couple whom I had counseled many times as they struggled with the fact that they could not have children. They were facing the decision now of whether or not they should adopt. Their shoulders were drooped, and they appeared so fragile as they tried to determine what they should do.

I saw a couple getting out of their car and carefully helping the husband's mother to get out. Their youngest child had graduated from college just two years before and they had been making plans for their golden years. Then his father had died suddenly, and his mother had moved in with them. She had struggled for years with the unpredictability of multiple sclerosis and was unable to live by herself. I thought about the many adjustments that we are called on to make throughout life.

I was filled with joy as I watched the many singles

hurrying into church. They have so much pep and enthusiasm and are a valuable asset to our church. Some of them still lived at home, others were just beginning to make their homes in apartments and condos throughout the city.

I hurried into the morning worship and looked out to see the families sitting together. It took time for them all to get ready to be in church. I am aware of the time it takes to get everyone ready, to find the socks and shoes, to get the hair brushed, all those things it takes for families to venture out. I admire and appreciate the young families that make this a priority and get to church and Sunday School together. It also makes me strive harder to provide the framework through church programs and worship for the nurturing and strengthening of these people who make the commitment and take the time to be a part of the church family.

One of my best friends has had and is having a productive professional life, but my admiration for him goes far beyond that. I admire him because when we are together, he talks about his family. He shares with me things they are doing, where they are going, little stories about their daily experiences. There is not a busier man in Atlanta, but he knows the value of family, and he takes time to be with them and to share with them.

After worship, I went back to my office and made several notes that have now become the framework for this book. No matter how you define your family, I hope you will find some words of encouragement and hope that will help you with the challenges and opportunities before you. I don't know how anyone can get through life without a close relationship with God. Through prayer and seeking his way, we can find only in God the strength and comfort to meet the challenges of the daily ruts and routines of living. He alone brings the hope for eternal life that makes it all worthwhile.

I

What Is a Family?

ONE DOES NOT GET VERY FAR into thinking about families of today without realizing that the definition of "family" has changed — and expanded.

Single-parent families have one parent as breadwinner, caregiver, mother, and father, all rolled into one demanding, sometimes exhausting role. Single parents are on duty twenty-four hours a day, every day! And when the day is done, in the quiet hours of the night, there is no one to share the joys and problems of parenting.

Two-career couples face the endless conflicts of trying to balance work and family. Many statistics show that at least 52 percent of women whose children are under age three are in the workforce. This cultural phenomenon has a profound effect on our children, who need parents available emotionally as well as physically.

Another aspect of family life today is the growing number of stepfamilies, or as some say, the blended family. More and more of our children are being raised in families where one of the natural parents is not present daily. In that situation the stepfather or the stepmother has a large role in the day-to-day guidance of the child. So, in fact, these children are learning to deal with two families. We are learning more every day about the impact that can have in families' struggles to be healthier and happier.

So however you define a family, today's families are experiencing tremendous pressures and stresses! Families of all sorts still must cope with chronic illness or the everyday stress and strain of making ends meet. Mark Novack, a Catholic theologian, has said that to be a family in this day and age is nothing less than an act of courage, and I agree.

Parents face tremendous pressures and must work through many. I'm encouraged by the fact that most of the parents I know have a passion for wanting to do a great job! They are vitally interested in facing whatever their family's problems might be, and they seek to maintain a wholesome and healthy family life. As we look at some of those problems here, I want you to note those qualities of family life that promote strength and wholesome values.

It is through recognizing the problem areas of family life that we can be forearmed and prepared. The pressures facing families today are accentuated by several realities:

+ *Divorce.* One of the major realities of life today, divorce claims half of all marriages. Sixty percent of all second marriages are ending in divorce. The sad reality is that many couples who one day said "I do" are standing before judges with greater frequency and are saying "I don't want to anymore!"

  Many times I have married three or four couples a week. More than a hundred people a year have stood before me to say "I do," "Yes, I will," "I want to," or "I'm eager to." And they mean it!

Some will say about marriage: "That's a risky thing to do!" You bet! But without the risk, there is no royalty; without the reaching and striving, there is no capturing and achieving.

I can tell you that many of the people I have married are in a state of fantasy. You don't really get to know each other until your heads are resting upon the same pillow, until you are drinking your coffee out of the same pot, until you are brushing your teeth over the same lavatory — and there you are. It's like living in a room full of elbows. Marriage is the most intense form of human fellowship, and you find out things about each other that neither of you ever dreamed about. Some of these discoveries are wonderful; others will drive you up the wall! It's in this arena that you live out this promise — the commitment of your wedding vows.

Someone once told me, "My wife and I are incompatible." What's the big deal about that? No two human beings are perfectly compatible. You just work together to be happy and have a fulfilling life in spite of those incompatibilities. You make a commitment to one another, and you seek a way through, rather than a way out.

I walked through the receiving line at a fiftieth wedding anniversary celebration and talked with the couple celebrating half a century together. The husband said to me, "We've never had a cross word with one another, preacher." He lied! If he didn't, one of them is a zombie. Never a cross word? Let's not kid one another. You have to work at it, and you work at it because you made a promise, you made a commitment.

Society doesn't support your working at it. Society doesn't say, "Work your way through." It says, "Listen, life is too short — get out." And many do. That's one of the things that is changing the face of the family, leading to divorce and the creation of single-parent and stepfamilies.

• *Single parents.* Some single parents, of course, are single because a spouse has died. But many single parents have never been married, and I have seen that with greater frequency than you might imagine. Recently a young woman, pregnant and unmarried, asked me if I would baptize her baby when the baby came. I promised her I would, and I did. I asked my congregation to stand in support of the Christian nurture of that child. You see, that child is a child of God, and I would never place any condemnation upon that innocent child.

• *Two-career couples.* More and more we see families where both parents are working, either through necessity or through desire. I simply don't know how they do it! They must be under a constant strain, torn and pulled between duty and desire, between the demands of career and responsibility as parents.

There must be questions that grip their every thought: Do I have it within me to give my best to both career and family? How can I cope with the guilt of having to leave my children with someone else? When is it OK to leave my baby? As a father, am I ready to step in and help with the nurturing of this family since my wife is now helping me provide for the basic needs?

There are surely heart-wrenching questions that must be faced by those families in which both parents are working outside the home. Believe me, I am not condemning those parents. I know there are many cases in which two incomes are absolutely necessary. But regardless of the reasons for parents working, two-career families face problems and questions that strike hard at the very core of today's family.

- *Stepfamilies.* Often there is bitterness between the natural parents in two sets of stepfamilies, and this can be played out in the handling of the children.

There are complications over visitation, many arguments over money, and difficulties with relationships with the stepparent who may even bring his or her children into the home. As children grow older and are involved in their own activities, strains and stresses are encountered when they resent having to give up something they really want to do because it is visitation time with mother or father.

All of these realities and challenges affect the children and family, and they bring about conflict and stresses that just didn't exist in the days of our grandparents.

We all have our ideal of what the family should be, what we hope it will be, and what we want it to be. I think all of us have Robert Frost's view of home: that place where they have to take you in when you get there!

Our family should be a haven, a place of respite, and a place of acceptance. It should not be a battleground, a place of intense competition, or an arena of stress. It must be a place of rest, of renewal, where together the family faces life united and with love's resources assembled!

Rejoice!

There needs to be joy, experienced and expressed in the family circle. Someone once asked what I was teaching our grandchildren, and off the top of my head I replied, "To experience joy!" I want them to think of their grandfather as one who loves them deeply and as a person who is fun to be around. If they experience joy in my presence, they will listen to the lessons that I will surely teach them. Children — indeed, entire families — need experiences of joy to shape and nurture them. One of the best ways to have and live with a sense of joy is to be thankful.

Spend time together!

Spending time together is very hard to do in this hurried-up, revved-up society of ours. If a family is to be healthy and strong — if children are to be prepared for life and relationships — a family must spend time together. Our two daughters are both now grown. We spent a lot of time together as they were growing up, but I wish we had spent more. I treasure the memories of mornings when I would take one or the other of them to school. Those mornings were times of learning more about the makeup and character of that particular child. My daughters and I have since treasured the times when we could reminisce about childhood days and talk over plans for the future.

When my wife, Sara, and I reflected on the years of our daughters' growing up, the beautiful memories have included family trips, vacations, movies, lunches, and times of sharing around the table as we sat down together for meals. How many families sit down for meals together today? That is one tradition I wish would never be replaced. You can learn so much about your children, they can learn about you, and it is a wonderful time for interaction at the end of a busy day.

Let me remind you that the formative years of the life of your children pass but once. You have one chance and one chance only to make them good and memorable years. You need time to just talk, to laugh, to share your dreams, to plan outings, vacations. You need time to resolve conflicts, to be there to listen, to affirm, to appreciate! It takes time to do all of that in a productive way.

It is so easy to get caught up in the work of making a living that we don't take the time to live. Because the very makeup of today's family is changing, the role of the father as a nurturer is being given more attention today. When Woodrow Wilson was president of the United States, he said, "It's an awful thing to be president of the United States. It means giving up nearly everything that one holds dear. The presidency becomes a barrier between a man and his wife, between a man and his children."

Friends, you don't have to be president for that to happen! It can happen to any busy person driving for the top — reaching for his or her dreams. Before you know it, there is no time for anyone who needs you. It takes time — quality, persistent, regular time — for a family to be healthy and hold together in the face of today's stresses and challenges. Everyone in the family has to be committed to giving time to each other.

Respond to and praise each other

Family members help one another meet the challenges and choices of life. There should be no doubt in anyone's mind that they are cared for, loved, appreciated. Families who care about each other show it, they express it, they respond to each other with expressions of love and appreciation. I mean hugs! I mean kisses galore! We do a lot of that in the Harrington family. I will never forget the first time our son-in-law Harold came by the house when he and Vicki returned from their wedding trip. I, of course, kissed and embraced her and then intuitively embraced him. He had joined the family; he had become one of us.

Love needs to be expressed; it needs to be verbalized. We need to say "I love you," "I appreciate you," "I am proud of you," "I think you are doing a great job!" We dwell too often in the family circle on the negatives. There is a tendency toward too much nitpicking. It seems that every family has someone whose sole purpose in life is to keep everyone straight, and so a family reels from such a tart and biting tongue; each person is bruised by the words that come from that critical and censorious spirit! That should not be. We should be careful lest we be like the man looking at a garden who saw nothing but the weeds, amid flowers that were in full bloom.

Watch mixed signals

Some families seem to have a legacy of "keeping one in his place," and so the approach to each other might be described as, "Love one another, but don't say it. Affirm each other, but cut each other down to size. Compliments should always be followed with a stout dose of humility." In that environment, one hand seems to bless; the other seems to take it away!

Sometimes even our praise is a put-down. A child brings in a test score of 98, and the mother or father says, "Fine, but next time make it one hundred." What impression does the child get? The child leaves thinking, *No matter what I do, they cannot be satisfied; I can never please them.* If you are not careful, you will put that child on a treadmill — one of trying to please everybody — that he will be on for a lifetime!

Love unconditionally

I cannot emphasize enough the importance of having and showing unconditional love in the family. Surely there are times when we are disappointed in the actions of our spouse, or the children. But through it all, there needs to be the thread of unconditional, unqualified love. That is what holds the family together.

This assurance of caring and loving helps families face the crises, the conflicts, and the cruel realities of life. In every life, in every family, there will be some good and some not so good; some praise and some pain; some triumphs and some traumas. Reality must be dealt with in the family. James Baldwin was talking about reality when he said: "Not everything that is faced can be changed; but nothing can be changed until it is faced."

It is in the family that we teach each other how to face the world. Healthy families are able to confront reality. They realize that failure is not the end of the world; it may, in fact, be a stepping-stone to something better. Trouble should not destroy the family; it should strengthen it.

A common faith

We need each other's love and affirmation to make it in today's world, and I firmly believe that the family needs to have a foundation of spirituality, a common faith.

How does one face the issues before the family? How does one find the answers to the many questions of rearing children nowadays? How does one gain the strength to bear the problems, the burdens, and the many responsibilities of life? There is only one way, and that is to place your trust and hope in God. We must believe in the One who can give us the assurances that we need to meet life's challenges, and by having faith we can get through.

Faith is taught primarily in the family circle. Spiritually, we cannot give our children what we do not have. You cannot teach your child the value of truth if you constantly present a picture of falsehood. Someone has said that in the home religion is more caught than taught. We can talk to our children about love, compassion, and concern for each other, but if the example they see is our constantly running roughshod over people, then our words have not impact because of the erosion of our example!

Our Muslim brothers and sisters are zealous about the faith; they are teaching it to their children, and they are reaching out to others. What are we doing? Many of us sit with the expectation that someone else will teach our children. No one will teach them much without your support and your efforts at home every day.

Families should be united, undergirded, and sustained by a common faith. It is troubling to me that we often do everything for our children but provide them with spiritual direction. We are often more concerned about their secular education and social acceptance than with spiritual awareness and development.

Think of Norman Rockwell's classic painting *Sunday Morning.* Walking toward the door, dressed for church, is a mom and two children. With Bible in hand, the three well-groomed family members are marching across the room, single file, headed for the door. But to get to the door they have to navigate around a man, unshaven, in bathrobe and slippers, sitting in all of the clutter of the morning paper. The picture is obvious. Sunday means something far different for him than it does for his wife and two children. They will be sitting in a pew during worship, he will be sitting in an easy chair at home. They will be reading their Bibles, he will be reading the comics and the sports page. They will follow the church bulletin during worship; he will be searching for the television schedule. It is Sunday morning, and the painting tells of a family divided, not united — and they are worlds apart.

The example of the father at home will make an impact — a powerful impact on the children as they grow. Thank God for a faithful mother who is doing what she can.

As I look out on society today, I see the picture Herman Melville describes in the novel *Moby Dick,* when he tells how out in a calm sea, far from any shore, the whaling ships would often lower their sails and drift along and allow the crew members to leap overboard, to swim awhile, to take a bath. "Now, in calm weather, to swim in the open ocean is as easy to the practiced swimmer as to ride in a spring-carriage ashore. But, the awful lonesomeness is intolerable. The intense concentration of the self in the middle of such a heartless immensity, my God! Who can tell it? Mark, how when sailors, in a dead calm, bathe in the open sea — mark how closely they hug their ship and only coast along the side."

Isn't that a picture of life as it is for so many today? We feel as if we are adrift, so many feel abandoned and lost! We just need to have something to nestle up close to and hug! That's what the church is — a great ship of spiritual vitality that embraces all of us. Through fellowship with those who are struggling and experiencing life's trials every day, just as you are, you can find strength and comfort. Through worship you can feel nurtured and gain the inner peace and calmness needed to wade through the routine of everyday.

We need to reach out to each other, to hold hands, to look up and ask for God's help and strength! That's the only way today's family — in whatever form — can make it through.

II

Single
Parents:
I Salute
Them

BY AND LARGE, you do not become a single parent unless some trauma is involved.

A pregnant young woman decides to keep the child, intending to give the child hope and opportunity. She will need a great deal of help and support.

A spouse dies, and a mother or father, left alone with the children, must deal with the grief.

A divorce occurs, custody is given to one or both parents, help is needed. Divorce is, in fact, a grief experience because a relationship has died. The adjustment is greater in a sense because the corpse is still walking around.

And more frequently we are finding the single parent chose to have a child, and to raise that child, alone.

A legitimate question is being raised in America today: Where are the fathers? In nine out of ten single-parent homes, it is the father who is missing. One fifth of all American children live in homes without fathers.

Single parents, for the most part, do not really seek this demanding, oftentimes impossible, role; it is usually thrust upon them in some way. The ache of grief, the loneliness, and in some cases feelings of betrayal have to be worked through before these individuals can come to find a sense of wholeness and healing.

If you are a single parent, be sure that your children get the help they need to make the necessary adjustments to a death or divorce. In many ways, children often suffer more than when a parent dies; even after ten to fifteen years the wounds of divorce are still considerable.

In this time of great adjustment, you must ask for the help and support that you and your children need. You might ask, "I can just barely afford to put groceries on the table, how on earth can I pay for counseling?" Many agencies can provide this guidance for minimal fees or even for free, but I believe the best place to begin is with the church. Most ministers provide free counseling, and if you need long-term help, they can refer you to those organizations, agencies, or support groups that can provide the long-term healing therapy needed.

If you are not already active in a church, get active! With the fellowship and support of Christians surrounding you, you should find the framework needed as you search for help in adjusting to the circumstances that thrust you into the role of single parent.

In Luke 11:9, we find these words: "Keep on looking, and you will find." I think there are some things that parents — whether or not they are single — should be seeking.

Seek to be the best parent you can be

I can only be amazed at the demanding nature of the single parent's role as breadwinner, nurturer, mom, dad, and car-pool director, and that is only the beginning. I want to pay tribute to the diligence and caring of single parents I have seen meet the incredible demands of being a good parent.

The statistics are staggering. The United States Census Department, in 1998, reported that almost 30 percent of all American families are single-parent families. A huge percentage of today's newborn children will spend some time growing up in a single-parent home.

One of the best books I have read on the subject of single parenting is *One on a See-Saw: the Ups and Downs of a Single Parent Family,* by Carol Lynn Pearson. You get the message quickly that one person on a see-saw is not much fun; in fact, it will not work with one person.

Pearson recognizes the challenge, and she is doing the best she can; it is all anyone can do. The qualities that make for good parenting — being available, being willing to spend time, doing things together — are obvious, but the challenge is greater for the single parent. Time at home is generally limited. It usually is up to the single parent to provide for the necessities at home, and combining a career with parenting makes enormous demands on one's time and energy. We hear a lot today about quality time, and that is even more of a rare commodity to the single parent.

Seek to build up your children!

"Love is the best way of them all," wrote Paul. Love that is unconditional, that encourages, and that affirms is still the most decisive influence in the life of a child. If you don't do anything else for your children, giving them such love is more important than a vacation at the beach or the very latest in video games. It puts something into their hearts that lets them know they are someone of worth. It's not always easy to convey unconditional love to your children, because if your children and grandchildren are like mine, they sometimes reveal a fair amount of what I call "original sin."

When one of our girls was very little, I had experienced one of those days when everybody and his brother and sister and cousins and aunts and uncles had been after me for something. By the end of the day, I felt like a chocolate chip cookie everybody had taken a nibble of, and I was looking forward to getting home. I planned to walk into the house, take off my tie, slip quietly into my study, and let my soul catch up with the rest of my body. I anticipated with delight a time to just relax!

But it was not to be. When I arrived, there stood one of my daughters in the carport, lined up with three of her friends, gathered in solemn assembly. I noticed she had a little shoe box under her arm, and I wondered what was in it. I parked the car, and when I got out, my daughter said gravely, "Daddy, I'm so glad you are home. I promised my friends that you would do something."

"What is it you want me to do?" I said.

She looked up at me with those wide, innocent

eyes and replied, "Have a funeral for this dead frog we found!"

Now can't you just see the picture? Here I am trudging down through the woods before this little group. I am not only the preacher, I am also the funeral director and the gravedigger. It's the first time I ever had a funeral where I carried the shovel with me. Of course, this frog had to die in the middle of the driest part of the year, when our Georgia red clay is packed harder than a rock. And that frog was thrice dead. I could have picked it up by one foot and tossed it like a Frisbee.

But I can assure you no frog south of God ever had a better funeral. I hugged everybody, and we had a prayer thanking God for all creatures great and small. I went to my study, my daughter and her friends were happy, and all was well. Many, many years later, her teacher told me about an essay in which my daughter had written, "I knew my daddy really loved me when he had a funeral for a frog."

Now think about that! What if I had said, "I'm too tired" or "Get that trashy thing away from me"? You never know when that special moment for showing unconditional love is going to come your way!

A child who is loved and encouraged is a child who has a sense of self-esteem and a healthy sense of self-worth. The "glory moments" of family are those moments when love is expressed. It might be just a little thing of the moment, such as burying a frog, but in memory's eye it can become a sustaining moment in time when the message was clear from parent to child.

It might be your presence at a soccer game. It might be a quiet OK when a mistake was made. It might be a hug at just the right moment. You never know when a moment of caring will make such an impact that it will be carried through the years as a special memory. Love should always be looking for the best to highlight, to build up, to encourage.

So if there is only one thing you can give your children, *give them love*. If they have love and encouragement, they will often find a way to attain the other things that really matter. From an inner sense of worth most things that are good will come.

Seek support from others — and from yourself

Everyone needs a circle of friends who will be supportive, caring, and honest with us. We all need friends who will stand with us, stick by us, and are forthright and reliable. It is a must for all of us and even more so for the single parent.

We hear a lot today about support groups, and friendship is what they are all about: people in like circumstances who have been through what you are going through, or who are faced with challenges you have already conquered. Paul Tournier said it best: "No one can develop freely in this world or find a full life without feeling understood by at least one person."

And seek some time for yourself! There is never a real letup for single parents, who never really finish.

We all need time for ourselves, to develop some perspective about what is happening to us, to look to the future and make some plans, to have a life that is private, and frankly to take stock and count our blessings.

If you are a single parent, you are probably even now thinking, *Preacher, that's all well and good. I would like to join a support group, and I would like to have someone with whom I can share, someone who understands me. But to have a friend, you have to be a friend, and right now, I don't even have the time to shave my legs, get a haircut, or do the countless other things that no one else can do for me. Just where am I supposed to find the time — not to mention the energy it takes — to invest in friendships and nurturing of myself?*

There is no easy answer to those questions. We all feel the press of never finishing, never getting things done. For your own self-esteem, as you prioritize your schedule, make some time for yourself! It will be a wise investment, not only for your sanity and well-being, but those moments spent wisely on yourself will help you cope and feel more self-assured as you face life's daily challenges.

Life is filled with surprises and disappointments, and we all need some perspective in our life. Life is what happens to us while we are making other plans. We have to deal with whatever comes our way and somehow make the best of it. So keep your perspective if you can and give thanks for the little things along the way. Find those few moments a day just for yourself, whether it means rising a few minutes early or slipping away for a moment or two before the baby-sitter leaves. Or ask another single parent to take your children for an evening, and do the same for her or him.

Seek and find a vital faith

Through your faith you can be sustained. Find yourself a church that can provide strength and nourishment to your spiritual life and your children's. Spiritual life is like every other aspect of your life. It is a cultivated relationship, a relationship on which one is continuously working. You need to be persistent, always asking, seeking, trying to relate, to find, to be aware of the will of God for your life. It does not happen overnight; it comes as the result of the steady habit of one's life.

Faith is the result of a cultivated relationship, and we need to be cultivating our relationship to God on a daily basis. Ask God to help you; ask friends to help! Seek answers and ways to cope with your responsibilities, and remember these words: "Keep on knocking, and the door will be opened" (Luke 11:9). It would be so easy in the face of challenges to just give up. Knocking is not merely asking, not merely seeking or searching, but an act. It raises a noise. It attracts attention.

I see such knocking in so many single parents. They just keep on keeping on, they learn to adjust and to cope. I see so many who then rise up strong, working day in and day out to provide the material things needed, but also persisting in their devotion to their children. I see them seeking to undergird their family with love, with respect, and with the values that never grow old.

So if you are a single parent, hang in there and ask, seek, and knock. With faith and persistence, you will make it through.

III

The Blended Family

Yours, Mine, and Sometimes Ours!

THE TERM "blended family" has overtones of something forced. Oftentimes when food comes out of a blender it looks like mush; in fact, it is mush. The dictionary defines the word *blended* as: "To mix ... to combine or associate so that the separate constituents or the line of demarcation cannot be distinguished ... to mingle intimately ... to produce a harmonious effect." *

The two phrases — "to mingle intimately" and "to produce a harmonious effect" — are what we are striving for in the ideal blending of families. "Intimately" implies that there is a willing, voluntary coming together. "Harmonious effect" suggests that the coming together has produced a sense of unity and happiness. As in all relationships that matter, love is the foundation of the relationship. In a blended family, two persons fall in love and desire to get married. Both have

*Definition reprinted by permission from *Merriam-Webster's Collegiate® Dictionary, 10th Edition.* © 1999 by Merriam-Webster, Incorporated.

children from previous marriages, and two families actually come together.

In such a stepfamily, one or both parents bring a child or children into the marriage. This structure can be further strengthened, or further complicated — you can take your choice — by the couple's having a child, or children, that is uniquely their own. So in reality the family then can become "yours, mine, and ours."

I was once at a social occasion and saw two long-time friends. Both had lost their spouses and remarried each other. I was delighted about their marriage and listened with amazement as they told about their family. Together they have eight grown children. Each of those children is married, and among them, they have thirteen children of their own. When the family gets together, they begin with thirty-one people. Now *that* is a blended family!

Those who have experienced a blended family know that it is not easy. It is an enormous challenge because of all the diverse factors. Many kinds of tensions can develop; there are complications in this setting that some nonblended families do not experience.

An equation of interrelationships involves one or more former spouses, and these relationships may be friendly or unfriendly. Last-minute changes in plans, late payment of child support — the list of sources of conflict goes on and on. There is the issue of grand-parents who naturally love and want to see their grand-children and relate to them. All of these complicating factors tend to cast a shadow of concern, if not a cloud, across every kind of family occasion.

It is a challenge, to say the least, because when you marry a person with children or both parties have chil-dren, you are marrying a package that involves all of these potentially complicating and conflict-producing possibilities.

Patterns of blended families

There are some patterns of blended families that, quite frankly, produce challenges not that different from the challenges facing any newlywed couple, with one caveat — all the responsibilities of family just come quicker and with a more diverse package of challenges.

One pattern I note in all couples who marry is that they launch their journey with expectations. Oftentimes when I have met with people who have had a marital difficulty, they said something to me like, "Now as I look back, I am not sure whether we were ever in love." That may be what the person is experiencing in her reality at the moment, but the statement is not true. Without exception, I have met with the prospective bride and groom before performing their wedding ceremony. Both bride and groom are eager with expectations for the future. At that time they profess their love for each other, and they have high hopes of having a successful and happy marriage. People launch their life together with a sense of joy and expectation.

Even those who are marrying for the second time are joyous and filled with eager expectation. I have had just a few weddings where it is the third marriage. These are somewhat more subdued in tone. When there are children involved, there is usually greater joy and expectation because the children are often so glad that new happiness has come for their mom or their dad, and they are anticipating better times ahead for their new family.

So every marriage is launched with high hopes and great joy. Then what happens? Some expectations are not met. As a matter of fact, some expectations were unattainable from the beginning. In many ways courtship is a kind of fantasy time. We often do not say all we mean or mean all that the other thinks we are saying. See if you recognize any of these conversations that took place during courtship.

She says: "Honey, I just love the out-of-doors!"

He thinks: *It's going to be great to be with her at 4:30 in the morning in a duck blind. It's damp and cold, but it will be great for us to share the great out-of-doors!*

She thinks: *Isn't it wonderful that we will be able to visit all of the great gardens of America together, and here in Atlanta we can spend many pleasant Saturdays at the Botanical Gardens!*

He says, as she picks up a tube of toothpaste at the drugstore: "I just love to go shopping with you."

He thinks: *She is so decisive; she knows what she wants. She just marched in here and picked up the toothpaste she wanted. Didn't take five minutes.*

She thinks: *I'm so glad we are so compatible. I have a hard time making up my mind about clothes and colors. The thought of him spending the day with me going from store to store, mall to mall, until we get the right things just thrills me!*

Is any of that familiar? You can just forget it! She does not want to sit in that duck blind before daylight. He does not want to go from store to store, from mall to mall. Courtships often set us up for disappointment. We do not always say what we mean, or the person to whom we are talking thinks we mean something entirely different. So some expectations are not met.

Examining roles in blended families

Once expectations can give way to reality, a time of examination sets in. In fact, to some degree this is an ongoing process.

That's because we are constantly changing, interacting, and examining the things that are basic to any family, but turn out to be complicated in the context of a family that's blended. In all families we look at the larger family of which we are a part! This is complicated in the blended family because the "larger" family is a different set of folks for each side of the husband/wife relationship. There are usually two ex-spouses that have to be considered, and if they have remarried, two other individuals and two sets of grandparents. I frequently have seen all the tension this can cause at weddings, which produce logistical quandries that a room full of auditors could not untangle.

Just think about all of this for a moment. In a blended-family situation where two sets of children are involved, all living in the same house, think of just some of the questions to be resolved: a fair distribution of space, fairness in rules for bedtime, consistency in allowances, chores to be done, and use of family cars.

Add to all of that the reality of former spouses along with the normal adjustments the couple has to make just to being married, and there will come times of examination. Many couples begin to wonder after marriage if their union will last, and if anyone has these second thoughts, I suspect they come to blended-family couples more quickly.

A lady once came to see me one day right after Thanksgiving. She had children from a previous marriage and had married a man with children. The recent holiday had brought all of them together, along with relatives from both sides. She told me, "As I looked out over the lawn and saw all those people engaged in a game of touch football, I thought, *Who are all these people?*" And then she said, "I don't even know all these people well, and some of them I do know, I don't like! What am I to do?"

I told her. "You just must learn to love them — you are married to all those people now!" Families, in fact, are happier when they can open the circle of love and make room for one more. What a joy it is when children of blended families can have the feeling of just being loved by more people, of having two sets of parents that love and care for them, and a large, extended family of grandparents and relatives that make each child, and each parent, feel welcomed and loved.

There are so many variables in blended-family finances. If child-support payments are involved, are they paid on time? It is sad to think about it, but many, many fathers do not make their child-support payments — on time or ever!

Money — the lack of it, the fair distribution of it — can play a big part in the struggle to bring harmony to the family. One set of children may be used to a higher standard of living than the other. Material things can be considered luxuries by one parent and necessities by the other. Some children require more money for health care, braces, eyeglasses, and such than others, and this can be a challenge.

Then there is the role of the stepparent. I do not like that prefix, "step." Is this someone to be stepped on? Or is this the person who does the stepping on? I have seen it work both ways. Stepparents have arrived at a great place of wisdom when they realize they are not the natural parent, but someone else. It does not mean that being a stepmother or stepfather is not a role where you can be significant, but it does mean that you cannot be more than you are.

Much has been written about stepparents, and in many ways they have been stereotyped as being "bad." It is often hard for the natural parent to accept that her child will be guided, or disciplined, by a stepparent. We've all heard the story about the mother who called to the father to come quickly because "your child and my child are beating up our child." All this can be quite confusing and complicated, but it can be worked out. It takes determination, it takes respect, and it takes love and commitment, but I have seen blended families who have overcome these challenges, and who have created an atmosphere of happiness and enthusiasm.

A happy marriage involves so many issues of acceptance, of really getting to know the person you have married. You have to accept each other's peculiarities and learn genuine love for the person you have married — and, in the case of blended families, the package that goes with your new spouse.

IV

Too Much
or Too
Little?

*What We Must
Give Our Kids*

AS PARENTS, WE KNOW that it is not easy to grow to freedom, and we constantly seek answers to the challenges of raising a family in today's world. We ask, are we giving our kids too much or too little? The answer is that we are giving our children too much of some things and too little of essential things. We must accept the reality that our children are growing up caught between these two extremes.

There is mounting evidence that middle- and upper-class Americans overindulge their kids. Rightly used, the material blessings of life can get your child off to a good start in life. But wrongly used, to the point of overindulgence, they will not be blessings but a blight that robs your child of the joy of anticipation, looking forward to attaining something that she dreams about. It can stifle incentive and the need to work for some things.

If children have everything too soon in life, then they can be bored with life before they are twenty. And let me tell you that boredom can lead, and often does lead, to a multitude of problems.

Some parents push their children too fast, too hard, and too far. I know of a family who started their six children in Little League just as soon as they were old enough for T-ball. Every year throughout football, softball, basketball, and baseball seasons they were all there. The parents served as team mother or coach of a team of players or cheerleaders. The children began cheering or playing ball before first grade. It seemed a good time for the children and parents to be involved together. There was rarely a day that they were not all together at the ballpark.

But an interesting thing happened. By the time the boys made it to high school, they were tired of the regimen of practice or games almost every day of the week. They had experienced the thrill and fun and were bored with it all. Their parents talked with me about their fears that they had pushed their children into these activities too early, and their childhood days had gone by without the quiet times of play and make-believe that they had experienced.

Now I am not saying that you shouldn't be involved in organized sports. I am saying that it is important for children to have time to play their own games, to develop and grow, and just do nothing.

Love your kids and accept them. Some kids are made for football and take to it; others go for the violin, so let them! Some want to paint; others want to dribble a basketball. You cannot make a linebacker into a ballet dancer. It takes love in the family circle to create an arena where children can be all that God meant for them to be.

I am convinced that a great many of our children today generally have too much too quick. Consider carefully your answer to these questions:

• *Am I giving my children too much freedom?* Have I undermined their discipline and moral guidance?

- *Does my child have too many material things?*
  Am I providing these things for my child out of
  guilt, to make up for the time I should be spending with her?

- *Is my child or children under too much pressure
  to perform?* Too much pressure can result in developing an "underachiever," or a child with a low
  sense of self-worth.

- *Am I protecting my child too much?* As a result,
  am I preparing him or her too little for life?

- *Or, is my child too independent?* Am I providing the necessary practical advice and tools needed
  to deal with growing up?

The costs of overindulgence

I was not plagued with overindulgence in my growing-
up years. I marvel today that I can have an orange any-
time I want, for when I was a boy we had oranges only
at Christmas. This is a concept that most of today's
children cannot even comprehend.

Basically, I was taught three cardinal lessons:

1. *Whatever we have — health, material things, opportunity — is a gift from God.* All that we have and own came from God and ultimately belongs to God.

2. *Whatever we have, in terms of blessings, carries with it the responsibility to be a blessing.* A talent must be developed, and opportunity must be seized and responded to. I was taught from my earliest days, concerning money, to give 10 percent to God, to save 10 percent, and to spend the remaining 80 percent wisely and well to the glory of God. The Harvard Business School cannot improve on that in terms of financial advice.

3. *I was taught that the world did not owe me a living, and that hard work and right living would be rewarded.* I began to work outside of the family farm to earn money when I was twelve years old. I had extra jobs and have worked from being a Tupperware salesman to weighing tobacco in a

warehouse. I was a clerk in a grocery store, managed a meat market, drove a trailer truck, and bought and sold produce at the farmer's market. I worked my way through college, and between the end of my college days and my summer job at the beginning of seminary, I drove a cement truck here in Atlanta to earn some extra money.

Parents have the responsibility to teach, to model, and to instruct their children. Overindulgence teaches lessons that are basically destructive.

A part of the motivation for overindulgence is our neglect. Many parents of children today are absentee parents. Some are absent due to necessity — but they are absent nonetheless.

A University of Michigan study indicates that mothers who work spend an average of only eleven minutes each day, during the week, in meaningful activities with their children and only thirty minutes a day on weekends. Fathers who work spend even fewer minutes with their children: eight minutes a day during the week and fourteen minutes a day on weekends. What are the results of all this?

God, and God alone, will know the ultimate results, but some of the returns are already in. Children who are neglected, for whatever the reason, get bored, develop emotional problems, and get into serious trouble with sex or with drugs. They deteriorate physically from poor eating habits and no exercise.

Youngsters from every economic and racial group are adrift, and their troubles pose a greater threat to American security, prosperity, and ideals than any external enemy. What is the answer? How can parents meet the demands on our time and energies and find the middle ground between overindulgence and neglect?

We need to take a long, hard look at our lifestyles. We need to examine what we want for our children and what we are accomplishing. We must try to understand what our children need and realize that those needs are our responsibility.

Until your children reach the age of accountable maturity, if you can, stay at home. If you have a choice, give your children the stability and security of growing up in a home where a parent is always there for them. If you have no choice, make the commitment to provide a loving, structured, safe environment for your children while you are away.

We need to provide a climate that promotes normal growth. As our children grow, they should be encouraged to eat properly, exercise, and keep themselves fit. Teach your children good habits of health and physical fitness. You cannot allow your children to become "couch potatoes" and expect them to be physically fit.

I won't delve into the horrors that can crowd their young minds as they spend hours watching senseless acts of crime, unbridled sex, and the casual use of drugs and foul language on television. A steady TV diet can soon make our children believe these actions are acceptable behavior. We must provide a climate for normal physical growth, and for normal intellectual growth.

It takes time and commitment. It takes hard work. It does not happen by accident; it takes parental leadership. It takes parents modeling what goodness and righteousness are. It requires that we be good examples. If parents don't set a good example for our children, then we are eroding everything we hold dear. How often I have heard parents say:

- *"I've exposed my daughter to a variety of religious beliefs.* That way, she can make an intelligent decision when she gets older."

- *"I try not to impose my personal moral beliefs on my son.* He's got to develop his own philosophy and live his own life."

- *"I don't care what my child believes as long as he's happy."*

- *"I haven't been too dogmatic in teaching my children about moral values.* I'm afraid they may reject mine and have none."

I believe all of that is sheer nonsense! That approach does not produce spiritually mature children;

it produces spiritual weeds. Parents must heed the examples we are modeling and setting for our children.

Our children must be taught the truths of right and wrong. They must be shown the true values of life by our example, so that as they become teenagers and have a life of their own they have the foundations needed to make the right decisions. They must be themselves, and we need to encourage their independence.

On the other hand, we can intimidate them, and they will never grow. They will never learn to fly for themselves, they will never come to that place where they can stand alone. It is a tragedy for both parent and child when that happens.

We should provide a climate for normal growth, a climate that nurtures independence, one that cultivates a larger purpose for life. We have not done much for our children if we do not put them in touch with a higher connection, if we are not helping them to develop a spiritual connection. Our children need to have a sense of "call" in whatever they end up doing in life.

Within the framework of our own special authenticity, we all should come to that point of awareness that our lives can count for something higher, that there is a larger purpose out there than "getting and spending and laying waste our powers."

It is this higher purpose, this higher calling, that is so essential to life. This calling keeps us going when the testing times come, and you can be sure they will come.

You must give your child something that is larger and more enduring than the mere things you can touch, handle, taste, and see. Home is where we get our values, good or bad! Home is where life makes up its mind about everything that matters — good or bad. Home should teach us not only who we are but also what we are. Home should teach us not only how to walk but also where to walk.

When I am gone, I will leave my children some of the artifacts of my life. But this much I hope, I pray — that they will have a faith to sustain them, a memory of how much I loved them. I want them to tell their children and their children's children that their grandfather, who was a preacher, was something of a character, but he loved his family, and he tried the best he knew to speak a good word for Jesus Christ.

Being a parent will take everything you've got — and more — of wisdom and compassion. It will take the help of God to see you through. As you struggle with the challenges and opportunities of providing the things that matter in the life of your family, remember just how important the influence of faithful parents can be. Focus your hearts and minds on being good examples, and pass the faith on to the next generation.

V

The
Challenges
Our Kids
Face

ALMOST EVERYONE agrees that the challenges facing our children today are far more formidable than the challenges we parents faced as we were growing up. Let's look at the reality in which our children are growing up.

The first thing our children will have to deal with, and deal with quickly, is the fact that we are living in a world of competition! That is probably not substantially new, but it seems to me that the competitiveness of our time has an intensity about it that is unique.

It seems to be a world, for example, with two contradictions. On the one hand, there is a great peer pressure — to dress the same way, sing the same songs, go to the same places. It begins early and becomes dominant in the teenage years. On the other hand, our children are growing up in a world of competition! It is a world where the unspoken message is the "winner takes all."

This means that our children are reacting to this world in either a hostile fashion or an apathetic fashion. Some become apathetic and do not choose to face the awesome demands for grades, blue ribbons, or trophies because they fear failure. Hostility comes from the conflicts that develop between them and their parents because of their apathy.

What kids need and desperately want is acceptance — acceptance from their parents for who they are. They want to be valued apart from trophies or the dean's list or high S.A.T. scores. If there is anything a struggling teenager wants to know, it is that he or she is special, loved, and valued by those persons they love the most! It is hard to come by that in a world dominated by competition.

Another part of our children's world, one of the strongest cultural currents that influences and sometimes drives us and our children, is consumerism. We no longer believe that old saying that a penny saved is a penny earned. We really believe that a dollar borrowed is a dollar spent! Consumerism is eating us alive.

We almost feel that it is our patriotic duty to spend, to buy. It keeps our economy humming. As a nation, we are spending more than we are taking in. We are constantly barraged with a steady drumbeat of persuasion to buy what we do not need, even if we have to go into debt to get it. Madison Avenue has convinced us that the things we do not have and really do not need are essential for life and happiness! Our children are bombarded daily through television with the message that there are things that one *must* have to be pretty, get dates, or be popular. We have even reached an era when television in our schools that is meant to be an aid to teaching has become an avenue for advertisements.

Ask yourself a question: Are your children, as they are growing up, becoming persons who will give more than they take, persons who will share? Are your children learning to be willing to serve? Or are they becoming persons who will simply wish to be served?

Our children are growing up in a world of chaos

— malicious mischief at best, a world of drugs, violent crimes, or vandalism at worst. Frankly, I would not trade the näiveté of my country upbringing for the shocking knowledge of what children are facing today! In this world, with its crisis of values, we should heed Alexis de Tocqueville's warning: "When America ceases to be good, it will cease to be great." I would add that when our country ceases to be good, it simply might cease to be. Sex is in and virginity is out, accompanied by a general loss of respect for self and little or no respect for others. Unintended pregnancy and abortion are rampant.

Finally, there is a crisis of home life that is creating many scars and dashed hopes for the next generation. If two people who are married take on the responsibility of bringing a child into this world, they are responsible for the well-being, the nurture, and the value development of that child. Many of our children feel like footballs, all kicked around and tossed about.

Our children are growing up in a world that is almost indescribable. The challenges before us as parents are immense. How can we respond?

A motto for any life

In the Bible we find Paul gave certain instructions to a young preacher, Timothy. I want to pass on those instructions as guidelines for facing life's challenges in this day. Paul said first to Timothy: Be a good example, hold on to your ideals! "Don't let anyone think less of you because you are young. Be an example to all believers in what you teach, in the way you live, in your love, your faith, and your purity" (I Timothy 4:12). Loving, loyal, and pure — a worthy, strong motto for any life.

Then Paul said to Timothy: Be a good student! It is a good idea for a young person to study his or her Bible. It is hard to get the lesson across, but the youthful years are years of preparation. The habits of study and discipline cultivated when one is young will likely be the habits of a lifetime! So we need to encourage our children to be good students of the Bible by reading it daily. We need to teach our children to pray and to prepare themselves in school and college to lead a useful and productive life!

Paul also advised young Timothy to be a hard worker. The best way we can meet the challenges of teaching our children the value of hard work is to work at being a good example every day of our lives. As parents, we must be thinking about the challenges before our children and ways to encourage and help them through these challenges every day.

Who decides about family values?

Make no mistake about it, you are shaping the future every day as mothers and fathers and grandparents. The values of your family are being decided at home, where the real priorities of our lives reveal themselves.

Someone in the family, ideally the parents, must give leadership to the family. If parents do not set limits for their children, offering a consistent manner of life and modeling what it is to be a good example of one of Christ's followers, a valueless vacuum develops. Everything that flows into that vacuum will be exceedingly negative.

Family values are not something you can run away from; you will pass values along to your children even if you are apathetic. You will give them a very clear message of indifference.

Your values in action

Teach your children about God — not only by actual teaching but also by example. Children receive not merely religious teaching from us but religious impressions as well. I would suggest:

- *Read Bible stories to your children.* One of my earliest recollections is of my mother reading Bible storybooks to me.
- *Say blessings before meals.* It is a natural and normal opportunity three times a day. You should never let a meal pass without this simple statement

of faith. It is also a way, early on, to involve your children in saying the blessing.

♦ *Pray with your children, and teach them to pray!* Participate in church as a family! Sit together as families in church. Be sure that when your child starts school, he or she is in worship on Sunday morning with your family.

You cannot teach your children about honesty if you are always cutting some corner. You cannot teach them about kindness if you are always being critical of someone and to them. You cannot teach them about love that is genuine if you are not practicing that kind of love. You cannot teach them about the joy of belonging to Christ if there is no joy in your life. You cannot make much of an impression on them about God's capacity to forgive if you are unforgiving!

One spring, our daughter Vicki and our granddaughter, Carolina, were with us. We put a quilt on the family room floor and Carolina, then an infant, played on that quilt. One afternoon, I was down on the quilt with her playing with her little toys, enjoying her. She threw away all the toys, you know how they do, and so she was just watching my hand. She reached up her little hand and caught mine. And in that moment I thought, *What a powerful transaction this is*, and I vowed a vow — that I would take that little hand for as long as I live and put it into a stronger hand, the hand of God!

Our children will very quickly be off our laps, but God forbid that they shall ever be off our hearts! We must walk hand in hand with them daily as we seek to teach them how to face this world of challenge.

VI

How Could One Abuse a Child?

IT WOULD BE almost impossible to write a book on the challenges and opportunities before the family today without looking into the subject of child abuse. Oh, what a painful subject it is; though it seems unbelievable, it is a reality in our world today. Rarely does a day go by that we do not read of these tragedies in our newspapers or hear on the television or radio news of another incident. As I worked on this book, it seemed that the subject of child abuse was dominating the news. There seem to be more and more senseless, unthinkable acts of abuse that we cannot even comprehend.

I love children. I have loved my own children with everything that I know. My grandchildren occupy a place in my heart that I could not even fathom before they arrived. Before Michael arrived, I wondered how I could possibly love another grandchild as I do his older sister, Carolina. He arrived kicking and screaming into this world, and with my first look, he captured a spot in my heart that is full of love and pride. Sara and I later experienced the joy of the birth of our third grandchild, little James, who is equally loved and appreciated.

The children at my church are all so full of inquiry and life. I frequently go by the nursery and spend time there watching the children play and interact with one another. Often I receive notes that they have written during church, and it is always a pleasure when they stop by my office just to say hello. I am deeply pleased that so many of them seem to know of my love for them and enjoy my attention.

Children are our future! Whenever a couple, out of mutual love, brings a child into this world it is a resounding vote of confidence in the future.

There is ample evidence in the Bible that our Lord loved little children. When the disciples would have sent them away at the end of a demanding day, our Lord said, "Let them come ... do not hinder them." He warned all of us of the dire calamity that would befall any who would "cause one of these little ones to stumble." So this chapter rises out of my love for children, but it also has its roots in the angst of reality — a reality that says, "How could anyone abuse a child?"

The silent epidemic

We must first acknowledge: it happens! It is happening within my own church, and chances are it will continue to happen. I have seen the bruises, the welts on their little backs and arms. I have noted broken bones and the battered little faces. I have observed the downcast eyes of fearful children, children who are afraid of the very persons that should love them the most — their parents!

We see it every day. Parents are indicted for abusing their children, children are taken into custody by appropriate authorities because they are being abused or murdered by their parents. Children are being killed by their parents — the ultimate abuse.

The number one killer of children under five is not accidents or crib death or leukemia. It is child abuse! Two thirds of all child abuse occurs with children under age four, with one third of that number being children six months old or less. It is estimated that one to three million American children will be abused this year, physically or sexually, and that almost 2,000 of those children will die. Almost 85,000 children were reported sexually abused in 1997. One in five girls and one in ten boys has been sexually abused before the age of eighteen, and in 90 percent of these cases, the victim knows the abuser.

It is a tragedy that is occurring daily across America, and by its nature it has not been talked about. The abused and the abuser often remain silent. The damage that is done is not only physical but emotional.

A happy childhood can fill us with pleasant, sustaining, nurturing memories for a lifetime. An unhappy childhood, an abusive childhood, can fill us with memories that bring pain throughout our lifetime. I know adults today whom I love and appreciate who are still trying to come to terms with and sort out the scars of childhood that impede the promise of their lives.

Child abuse goes beyond physical abuse. We abuse our children when we force on them our unfulfilled ambitions. We may project our own inadequacies on them. We may force them to grow up too soon and have to cope with things they are not equipped to handle. We abuse them when we verbally put them down or make them feel inadequate.

Reality is, we are abusing our children, and it must stop! As someone scrawled on a wall filled with graffiti, "Apathy Rules!" It often does; no one wants to get involved. No one wants to take a stand, no one wants to participate or make a move. We must first acknowledge that child abuse is a reality. It happens, and we must find ways to do something about it. Since most instances of child abuse occur within the home, we need to look at ways that we as parents can understand and prevent abuse in our own homes.

We do need to be sure that we understand the difference between discipline and abuse! I love to sit and read the Book of Proverbs, authored by Solomon. They are a source of amazing insight and practical wisdom. Two seem to be particularly helpful as we think about the subject of child abuse:

"If you refuse to discipline your children, it proves you don't love them; if you love your children, you will be prompt to discipline them" (Proverbs 13:24).

This gave rise to the popular saying, Spare the rod and spoil the child. Some have used this as a foundation for abuse, for excessive physical punishment of children. There is a fine line between too much and too little. To discipline means to teach, to shape, to give direction. We must furnish leadership as parents, and part of that leadership is consistent teaching at the point of discipline. Our family rules, values, or requirements must be consistent, or there is confusion in the minds of children. A child left without consistent direction, without affirmation, or neglected, at some point in time will bring shame to everyone involved.

How many times have you seen a parent telling a child, "If you don't stop, I'm going to ———"? The child continues whatever, and the parent again, and again, admonishes, "I'm going to ———." But the parent never follows through, and because the child knows nothing is really going to be done, he simply does not pay attention. Consistency in defining what is accepted behavior is important. Be careful in admonishing your children. Don't give idle threats or promises. Set limits and follow through on what you say.

Another helpful Proverb is, "Teach your children to choose the right path, and when they are older, they will remain upon it" (Proverbs 22:6).

In Hebrew, the phrase "train up" is an arresting concept. The original term referred to a rope that was placed in the mouth of a horse to give the animal direction. We must help our children find their own unique identities within the framework of who they are and who God meant for them to be.

I am sure you can think of parents who appear to be intimidated by the children and who are being led by whatever the child, or children, want to do. Parental leadership is essential in family life. A father-dominated family is generally a troubled family. A father-led family is generally a healthy family. Mother and father must work together to lead, to guide, to shape, and to train. This must be done within the framework of discipline, not abuse.

When I was a child, the punishment I received was to be switched. When I got older, my father would talk to me. I can tell you the talking was more effective than the switching. When our children were little, I spanked them, and when they got older, I talked to them. If I could do it all over again, even when they were little, I do not believe that I would spank them. I do not think it is the best way to teach — to give leadership. I pray that my children will remember more of my talks with them than the spankings I gave them. Children need to be disciplined. They need to have guidelines for acceptable behavior. But when they cross those lines, and they will, parents must seek ways of disciplining that are constructive — not abusive.

Now I am perfectly aware that there are times when it takes willpower to be loving and kind to one's child. I once encountered a young mother in the grocery store, obviously on her way home from work, and she must have just picked up her two young children. They all seemed tired and frustrated, and the children were letting her know they were ready to eat. In fact, they wanted cookies, candy, Froot Loops, marshmallows, and various other things. They kept putting these items in the grocery cart or pleading with Mother to let them have these items.

The mother kept telling the children, "No, we cannot get that today. Go put it back." After the mother had argued with them several times, one child pitched a temper tantrum, and a royal one at that. He began kicking, screaming, crying, and letting everyone in the store know that he wanted that item.

That harried young mother knelt beside young Johnny and tried in her soft, gentle voice to calm him down. By that time I was obviously watching and wondering how she would handle that situation. She told the child that she was very disappointed in his behavior. She then picked up the item, replaced it on the shelf, and went on about her shopping. When the youngster realized that he would not get his way, he amazingly hushed, and they completed their shopping. It takes a lot of self-discipline for parents to discipline unruly children.

There is no place in any family life, let alone Christian family life, for violence of any kind. The reality that we are becoming more and more aware of the problem is in itself a positive sign. As we work together to prevent abuse I would suggest the following:

- *If you are an abuser,* if you are a child that is being abused, don't keep silent: *ask for help. Get help!*
- *If you were abused as a child, you have a high potential to be an abuser.* Be conscious of this, and

get help before it happens to you and to your children.

- *If you have friends who seem to be growing more and more frustrated with their children,* inquire as to how you might help and give them a chance to share their feelings.

We must encourage our friends, we must encourage each other to concentrate on loving our children when they're good and loving them when they are not so good. In other words, we as parents must think positive! We must talk with our children. We must develop an atmosphere of trust where they feel free to talk things over with us without fear of judgment and admonishment. That is hard to do, but so important for your relationship. Encourage your children to tell you what is going on, to speak out if some adult is behaving strangely toward them.

So much of today is rooted in yesterday. Past hurts and shame hinder some of us from truly living in the present. But the love of Christ is bigger than your hurt, your shame. God does not want any of us to miss today because we are still trying to cope with yesterday.

We must all become more aware of the many ways in which we abuse our children. Most abuse is rooted in unrealistic expectations, unfulfilled dreams, and unresolved anger. It is incredible to me that families, people who live in such close proximity, can be so far apart and perceive one thing as reality when reality is something far different. Some of those perceptions cling to us, clutch at us, weigh us down for a lifetime.

If you are an abuser, God will give you the power to get the help needed to overcome. Seek that help, now, today, and seek forgiveness from those you have hurt. It is my prayer today for your children, for all children, that by God's grace they may live the lives for which they were created — and that we as parents may be granted the wisdom to provide the comfort, hope, and joy our children need to sustain them in today's world.

VII

Don't Give Up!

Advice for Parents and Teenagers

IN MY CONTACT with parents, particularly as their children enter adolescence, they have conveyed to me concerns and a desire for help and hope. They know their children are entering their formative years in a challenging and even hostile environment. The teenage years often make parents think of giving up, and some do! The teenage years make the teenagers wonder if their parents are human, and some teens give up and run away from home.

One of the couples who came by to see me recently wanted to talk about their son. I will never forget their opening statement: "We have come through two years of pure hell with our son, and we are at the end of our capacity." The very same day, a young lady, in her teens, came by just to chat with me a moment or two. "I can't seem to get along with my parents anymore," she sobbed. "They don't understand me. I don't understand them. We fight all the time, and it scares me!"

Parents and teenagers do agree on one thing during this period: that the teen years put a strain on the family, on relationships in the home.

Look in your Bible at Luke 2:41–52. You will find there an appealing scene in the life of Jesus of Nazareth when He was on the eve of becoming a teenager. In this story we note several helpful things: his parents, along with other families, are on a religious pilgrimage. They are going to Jerusalem to observe Passover. We note here that they went "every year." It was the usual thing for them to do. The practice and observance of religion was the steady habit of his family's life.

Take a look at your religious life today, as parents. Take a long, hard look. What you are religiously, in the practice of your faith, is what your children are likely to be and become. We often make all kinds of excuses at the point of the religious training of our children, and the practice of our own faith, but let's be honest: what they are, friends, are excuses!

We can all make our excuses, but let the record

show that the parents of Jesus of Nazareth made regular practice of their faith. They went to Jerusalem for the observance of Passover.

When Passover was complete, his parents, traveling with others, were on the way home when they noticed that Jesus was missing. We might say, "Why didn't his parents know He was missing?" The normal, routine way of traveling then was for the women and children to lead the way, the men following along behind. The children moved constantly from one group to another, and so He was not immediately missed by his parents.

When they had been traveling a full day, they missed him. They discovered that He was not in the group anywhere.

Needless to say, they were frantic. They were a day from Jerusalem; it took a day to get back and a full day to find him. His mother, as any mother would be, was "greatly distressed." In fact, one translation has Mary saying a normal thing to her son, "Why have you done this to us? Your father and I have been very worried."

And they had reason to be worried. Some scholars indicate that as many as two million people would be jammed into Jerusalem at Passover time. A twelve-year-old boy had no business wandering around among two million people if his parents did not know where he was, who he was with, and why! They were distressed, and should have been.

But there was great relief that He had been found, safe, well, and in church (in his case, the temple). The story, which ends on a happy note, captures the ideal of what we want for our children. "So Jesus grew both in height and in wisdom, and he was loved by God and by all who knew him." It is what we hope for and pray for.

As you study carefully this unfolding family drama, it ends well, but it also reveals a pattern that I believe is helpful, particularly for those parents whose children are entering adolescence, and helpful for those children who are in the throes of adolescence and need to understand their parents.

The adolescent

Adolescence is a time when little boys begin to become young men, when little girls become young ladies. There are biochemical and hormonal changes that profoundly alter appearances and affect behavior.

There are emotional changes. The teen is sometimes way up, sometimes way down, but almost always negative as the generations collide. Parents have to accept that these mood swings are part of growing up and at the same time be observant enough to realize that there are times when these mood swings can be an alarm that help is needed. Teens of today are showing an increasing rate of depression. Parents need to be supportive, understanding, affirming, at times firm, but always loving. You need to stay in touch, to talk. It is easy to say and hard to do. Don't build any walls, don't burn any bridges, don't give up! A better day is coming for both parent and teenager.

There are social changes. Boys and girls begin to notice each other for the first time. They fear, above all other fears, the rejection of their peers. Parents, you must remember that it is more important to teens to have their peers like them than it is for their parents to be happy with them and their behavior, or with their appearance. They all seem to want to dress alike and fit in. Anything that threatens that ideal will cause intense conflict.

How do you get through it? Say "yes" as often as you can, and "no" when you must. It is difficult for parents to let go, to let their children grow and fail, but we have to give them their wings. We cannot smother them and be anxious over everything they do. These are the days when they learn who they are, how they feel about things. It is a time when teenagers will confront and challenge almost every value their parents stand for.

- *If the family does not drink,* teens will want to drink, and ask, "Why not?"
- *If the family does drink moderately,* they will want to test the outer limits of that and ask, "What is

too much? Who sets the limits?"

- *If the family goes to church,* they will not want to go, and if they do go, they will not be caught dead sitting with their parents.

Teenagers face challenges that we did not have to deal with in my teenage years. There is the challenge of drinking and drugs. Young people are into drink and into it big these days. It should come as no surprise to us because we have made the cocktail hour the centerpiece of much of our socializing.

So, granted that it is a decisive period, the question before us is essentially this: What can we expect during adolescence as parents, as young people? You can expect at least four things.

Curiosity

The teenage years are a period of questioning and learning. When Jesus of Nazareth disappeared from the caravan, his parents were upset. When they found him, He was at the temple asking questions. Oblivious to time, not even thinking about the worry of his parents, He was as curious as a boy from Nazareth would be in a teeming city like Jerusalem. One author has stated, "Adolescence is not so much a period of time as it is a process of development."

It is a time of curiosity. Teenagers are eager to learn, and they want to learn. They are curious about all of the things happening to them. They want to learn more about themselves. They are experiencing not only the physical changes but also changes in their emotions and feelings. They are filled with questions and are seeking their own answers. They are developing beyond the age where they feel their parents have the answers.

How many times have you heard of a young adult commenting on how dumb he thought his parents were when he was in his teens, and how much those same parents had learned by the time he had reached his early twenties? It is natural for teens to be critical. It is a typical thing being described about Jesus: "Three days later they finally discovered him. He was in the Temple, sitting among the religious teachers, discussing deep questions with them" (Luke 2:46).

We know from the stories He told that our Lord was observant. He was curious. He noted the beauty of the lilies of the field. He was aware of the falling sparrow. He saw a sower go forth to sow some seeds. He observed that a shepherd tended his flock with great care. His orientation was rural. He noted the beauty and balance of the common things of life.

Confrontation

When Jesus' parents found him, He replied, "Why did you have to look for me?" Now that is the kind of thing a teenager could say or would say. Behind that statement is a lot: "I can look out for myself." "Don't you trust me to do the right thing?" "What is all the fuss about?"

What we have here is a confrontation. His parents were upset, and they let him know it. His mother wanted to know, as mothers do, why He had treated them that way — disappearing without saying a thing!

I once witnessed a confrontation between a mother and her daughter. The girl had wandered off somewhere in our building, and her mother had been looking for her. They were about to be late for a dental appointment. When they finally connected, there was a rather heated exchange. The child listened and then blurted out, "Get off my back! You are always on my case about things."

It is often that way during adolescence: the parent feels the need to maintain closeness and control. Adolescents feel they need space, a chance to test their own wings, and make more of their own decisions.

From the parent's point of view, the word that describes it best is "contrary."* It means "opposite in character," "tending toward an opposing course." Then we find some additional words in the dictionary that enlarge upon the basic meaning: "restive," which suggests

---

*Definitions reprinted by permission from *Merriam-Webster's Collegiate® Dictionary, 10th Edition.* © 1999 by Merriam-Webster, Incorporated.

an unwillingness; "balky," which is refusing to proceed for no evident reason; and "wayward," meaning "irregularity in behavior." Does any of that sound familiar to any of you?

There are confrontations during these years. They are inevitable because responsible parents set responsible limits. The limits are necessary for a sense of security for the child, but the child will test, seek to eliminate or define differently every limit that is set. It is a part of his growth to test the limits.

Not to have limits, though, is to impair the growth of the child. It would be like letting the butterfly from the cocoon too early — the butterfly would never fly. It would be weakened and impaired.

Communication

It is more than interesting to me that when his parents found young Jesus in the temple, and when the confrontation between them was over, "Jesus went back to Nazareth with his parents and obeyed them."

Communication was obviously good between the boy and his parents. They had confronted one another in openness and honesty. There is every reason to believe that Jesus had a normal upbringing for a boy of his day. He worked in his father's shop. He shared the family responsibilities. He played with his friends in the village. He obeyed his parents.

With all of the confusion around and the upheaval within our society, a similar communication is a must. I would urge all parents, within the foundation of love, to be honest with your kids.

Be honest and open about your differences, honest and loving with your affirmation.

Communication requires openness and honesty, but it also requires consistency. Just think of the confusing messages we often send to our young people. We alternately hurry our children, we push them, and then we become inflexible, rigid, when they want to innovate.

It is important for parents to stand together in their

expectations, and their discipline, when the expectations are challenged. Don't let your teenager pit one parent against another. Talk over how to handle given situations and let your teenager know that these expectations are enforced by both parents.

It is also important to be confident. Believe in your children and let them know it. The history books are filled with stories about people who were overlooked by many before someone found that there was something special there; usually that something special was found by "encouragement." Be confident and encourage your children, love them, and care for them.

There also is no substitute for availability. You either will be available to your kids as they move through adolescence, or you will miss it.

Be an example: a mentor for your kids. You will model something for them no matter what you do, so make it something good. Your children will be a reflection of what they see and experience in your home.

Above all, be loving! As Paul wrote to the

Corinthian Christians, "There are three things that will endure — faith, hope, and love — and the greatest of these is love" (I Corinthians 13:13). It is always the greatest. Effective communication is always based on love. If a child is valued, he feels valuable. If a child is put down, he feels worthless.

Commitment

When Jesus' parents found him in the temple, He said, "Didn't you know that I would be in my Father's house?" He was already thinking through a central commitment of his life. Some scholars believe that this was the dawning in his own life of the special mission that was to be his. Some of the most significant commitments of life are made during these adolescent years.

In my own life I began to feel an inner urgency, leading me toward the ministry, by the time I was fifteen. It became a firm conviction by seventeen, and by age eighteen I was officially accepted as a candidate for the ministry. I have never looked back on that decision.

Some of the most significant decisions of life are made during these years — decisions of faith and vocation. A well-lived life is founded in the quality of the commitments we make.

I can tell you as a parent, and now a grandparent, that it takes a commitment to persevere to have a family and a satisfying family life.

The challenge is real in these years, the challenge of curiosity, confrontation, communication, and commitment. But keep the faith and stick to it, because you may come one day to that ideal which was said of Jesus. May it be said of your son or of your daughter that he or she grew physically, mentally, spiritually, and socially. No satisfaction in life can or will match the satisfaction of seeing your children doing well.

VIII

Promises That Every Parent Can Make

ONE SUMMER, I was walking on the beach, just enjoying the breeze, and a beautiful blond girl with gorgeous blue eyes, clad only in the tiniest of bikinis, caught my hand. She just looked at me and with a big smile said, "Hi!"

I hasten to add that she was about four.

She had a sand pail and a shovel in her other hand, and she wanted to know if I would help her with her project. We chatted for a moment about her plans. She was certainly ambitious, for she told me that she intended to put all of the sand on the beach in her pail. As we worked and talked, my mind went back to when my own daughters were that young. My, how the years have gone by!

As I looked back, I thought of many things that I could have done, should have done, as a father that I did not do, but I can tell you that I have few regrets. I have not been a perfect father, but I have loved my two daughters unashamedly and with joy. If I could today change them, there is nothing that I would have different about either one of them.

But as that beautiful little blond of four and I continued our digging, I found myself thinking over and over again, *If I could do it over again, what would I do?* I share with you now some of those thoughts, for the relationship between parent and child is certainly one that needs to be included in any study of relationships.

Granted, we all want the best for our children. As I looked back and asked myself if I could do it over, what would I do differently, I have come to believe that there are some promises I would make and that you could make as a parent that would enrich family life and benefit our children. What are they?

Unconditional love

It takes a lot of love to make good children, and I do not believe that there is any influence as great as the power of unconditional love. I once heard a person say that "you can do anything you want with a child if you love him enough."

More and more as I have observed people of all sorts, in all walks and conditions of life, I've realized that security and stability come not through money but through the quality of love they've experienced at home.

Love is the essential ingredient that makes a child good. Of course, there are times when punishment is called for, but even punishment must be meted out lovingly and fairly. Before you punish your children, ask, "Am I punishing my child for his or her sake or mine?" We should punish our children not to dispel our own hostility, but because — and only because — we love them and want their lives channeled positively.

Never say "no" if the answer could be "yes"

If you want your child to learn criticism, then let your child grow up in an atmosphere where constant criticism is the order of the day. It's obvious that children who are raised in a positive atmosphere develop better and more winsome and pleasing personalities than those who are raised where "no," "stop," "don't," and "quit" are constantly heard.

I remember one day when I found myself constantly saying to my girls, "No! You cannot use my pens just to draw and color with." "No! You cannot waste my paper that I use for typing sermons just to scribble and draw on." After several episodes like this one, it suddenly dawned on me: *What is the big deal about the pens and paper? These are creative children with inquisitive minds. They like to explore and create.* Then I walked into the den and said, "Hey, girls, use this paper and these pens and make something beautiful." They both looked at each other in surprise and said, "Mama, what's wrong with Daddy?"

You could illustrate the point that I am making in a hundred ways. I believe that we should promise our children, with great benefit for both child and parent, that we will say "yes" as often as we can.

We can promise our children to really be with them when we are at home. This has been particularly difficult for me, since I would tend to retreat very quickly to my study and work. All day long I coped with people, dealt with broken things, shared hopes and dreams, listened to complaints and problems. I needed to be alone and not to have anyone tugging at me.

But my family, as all families do, would need my attention. Thank God my girls persisted! They would come into my study, sit in my lap, and make me talk to them. I am a better person because of their love and persistence.

Over the years, I have tried to arrange my schedule so that when I get home in the evening, I can stay at home and not have to go out again. It is important for all of us to really be with our children and our family when we are at home. A minister friend of mine told the most appealing story about one of his families. The husband travels from Monday morning until Friday evening. The minister was chatting with the wife and mother of that home one day and talked about how difficult it must be for her because her husband was always gone. She replied, "It's hard, but I don't mind it because when he's home, he's really home!"

Those of us who live with demanding schedules and impossible people demands must remember that our family needs us, too.

Try to see things from your child's point of view

One Sunday as the Session met to receive new members, a little girl was walking around in the parlor. She was about two and just as happy as could be. But there she was, walking around and looking up at all of us. Someone leaned over to speak to her and asked, "What's the view like down there?"

That is a profound question. It must have been quite a sight for her to look up at all the adults in that room towering over her. Even if we cannot agree with our kids, we should listen and enter into their viewpoint and give evidence that we understand and sense where they are coming from.

Sometime back, I was visiting in a home, and a child came in and asked if he could go next door. The father replied that he could not, and his son, as all children tend to do, asked why. "Because I said so, that's why!" the father answered.

That is not a good answer, nor the way to handle your children. That kind of answer leads to anger, intense frustration, and, ultimately, rebellion.

Put our children's hands into the hands of God

The vows that we make on behalf of our children when they are baptized are among the most demanding vows I have ever read. We promise as parents "by every means of God's appointment to bring up our children in the nurture and admonition of the Lord."

Our children belong not merely to us as parents but also to God. He gave them to us. In giving them to us, He also entrusted us with their spiritual well-being and growth.

The most important way in which we teach our children about God is by our example. If Christ is real to you, He will be real to your children. If Christ influences your life, He will influence their lives. Nowhere is it more true than in the home that religion is not so much taught as it is caught. How I pray that my girls can always believe in God through me and my daily actions.

On a beautiful tree-lined street, a little girl was walking with her dad, and as they walked and talked, threw rocks at telephone poles, and picked a few flowers, night was suddenly upon them. The little girl drew closer to her dad and said, "Take my hand, Daddy, I might get lost!"

I took her little hand and vowed that night that I would, as best I could, put her hand into the hands of

God, who would always be "better than a light and safer than a known way."

All of us who are parents can promise that, can't we?

ABOUT THE AUTHOR

W. FRANK HARRINGTON spent a lifetime in service to Christ and community. Over his forty-year calling to the ministry, he preached 2,200 sermons, and as senior minister of Peachtree Presbyterian Church in Atlanta, the largest church of the denomination in North America, baptized 3,000 infants and 1,000 adults and performed nearly 1,000 weddings. He had been preparing *Hope for Today's Families* at the time of his death.

Dr. Harrington was the author of three other books: *The Seasons of Life, Seeking a Living Faith,* and *First Comes Faith.* A celebration of his life and work, *To Comfort, to Strengthen, and to Guide,* will be published in 1999 by Peachtree Presbyterian Church Press.